STANDARD LOAN

UNLESS RECALLED BY ANOTHER READER
THIS ITEM MAY BE BORROWED FOR

FOUR WEEKS

To renew, telephone:
01243 816089 (Bishop Otter)
01243 812099

THE SECRET LIVES OF TEACHERS

Poems chosen by Brian Moses

MORE SECRET LIVES OF TEACHERS

Poems chosen by Brian Moses

PARENT-FREE ZONE

Poems chosen by Brian Moses

ALIENS STOLE MY UNDERPANTS

Poems chosen by Brian Moses

Don't Look At Me In That Tone Of Voice!

Poems by
Brian Moses

Illustrated by
Lucy Maddison

MACMILLAN CHILDREN'S BOOKS

Another one for my daughters,
Karen and Linette.

First published 1998
by Macmillan Children's Books
a division of Macmillan Publishers Ltd
25 Eccleston Place, London SW1W 9NF
and Basingstoke

Associated companies throughout the world

ISBN 0 330 35337 3

7 9 8 6

A CIP catalogue record for this book is available from the British Library.

Printed by Mackays of Chatham plc, Chatham, Kent.

CONTENTS

Elephants Can't Jump

Elephants can't jump, and that's a fact.
So it's no good expecting an elephant to jump for joy
if you tell him some good news.
You won't make an elephant jump
if you sound a loud noise behind him –
elephants can't jump.
You won't see an elephant skipping or pole-vaulting.
It wasn't an elephant that jumped over the moon
when the little dog laughed,
and contrary to popular belief
elephants do not jump when they see mice.
Elephants, with their great bulk,
don't like to leave the ground.
Elephants and jumping do not go well together.

And perhaps it's all for the best,
for if elephants did jump, just think
of all the trouble they'd cause.
If all the elephants in Africa linked trunks
and jumped together,
their combined weight on landing
would cause a crack in the Earth's crust.
Just think if elephants were jumping for joy
every time they won the lottery
or welcomed baby elephants into the world,
they'd probably have a knock-on effect
and all the rest of us would shoot skywards
when they landed.

I'm rather pleased to discover that elephants can't jump...
The world suddenly seems that tiny bit safer.

JUMP!

All the Things You Can Say to Places in the UK

Always say 'Ta' to Leamington Spa,
say 'Have a nice day' to Whitley Bay.
You can shout 'What's new' or even 'Howdo'
to inhabitants of Looe or Crewe.
You can tell the whole story in Tobermory,
say 'Hi' to Rye and 'Right on' to Brighton,
or call out 'Let's go' to Plymouth Ho.
Talk through your dreams in Milton Keynes,
say 'It's all for the best' in Haverfordwest.
Always say 'Yes' when you visit Skegness
but only say 'No' in Llandudno.
Don't tell a lie to the Island of Skye
or say 'It smells' in Tunbridge Wells.
Don't talk rude if you're down in Bude
or start to get gabby in Waltham Abbey.
Don't ever plead in Berwick on Tweed
or say 'You look ill' to Burgess Hill.
You could lose your voice and talk with your hands
when you take a trip to Camber Sands,
but whatever you say just won't impress
the residents of Shoeburyness.

Back to School

A week after the holiday begins
and there it is, in every shop window in town,
'Back to School' – I ask you.
As soon as they set us free,
the shops are all telling us
we've got to go back again.

I don't want new clothes,
I don't want new pencil cases,
I don't want new maths equipment,
I just want to be left alone,
I want to be on holiday
and not reminded how
in 4 weeks, 5 days, 7 hours, 39 minutes and 13 seconds
I'll be back at school.

And in one shop they even spelt it
'B-A-K.'
Well I reckon the people who wrote that sign
ought to go back to school too,
so they can learn to spell properly.
And here's what I say
to all those places that tell me
it's 'Back to School' –
'Back off – will you?
It's my holiday!'

My Brother's Girlfriend

My brother's girlfriend thinks *I'm* weird!
I showed her my collection of dead woodlice
and the hairs from Dad's beard, but she said,
'Ugh! You're disgusting.'

But what I say to her is, 'I'm different.'
Any kid can collect coins or stamps
but me I'd rather collect
ear wax,
toenail clippings,
squashed spiders
and chewed bubblegum
that's been left under tables.

And anyway, I don't think there's anything more weird than someone who *likes* snogging my big brother!

YUK! —

No Kissing

'Pupils at a Scottish boarding school have been warned not to get closer than six inches to a pupil of the opposite sex. Anyone breaking the rule will be disciplined. The rule is being introduced to stop children kissing and cuddling in the street.' THE TIMES

We've discovered kissing and it's really ace,
it's something you can do with your face,
but our headteacher said, 'No, no kissing.'
Can't somebody show him what he's been missing?

How much of a crime is kissing?

Are there degrees of seriousness?
What if you're aiding others to kiss
or loitering with intent to kiss,
'I didn't, I wasn't, honestly Miss!'

What excuses there'll be, and what allegations:
'I was giving her mouth resuscitation,
I thought she'd stopped breathing, she was turning blue,
I ask you, what else could I do?'

How much of a crime is kissing?

Teachers will be turning into spies,
'They were about to kiss, I saw it in their eyes.
If I hadn't been there and prevented this
there'd have been one huge explosion of a kiss.'

And will good teachers be rewarded,
the longer the list of kisses recorded?
What fun it will be to look and see
the names of those kissing illegally!

How much of a crime is kissing?

And won't it be good to take risks for a kiss
to do almost anything for a kiss
and on the day you're expelled from school
to boast that you broke the six inch rule,

to say that you broke it willingly,
for the sort of kiss that jellies your knees!

Elvis is Back!

Rumours persist in the press that the rock singer Elvis Presley faked his death. One of the most bizarre ideas is that Elvis was in touch with aliens and that they came down to Earth to spirit him away! One day, of course, he may decide to stage a comeback!

When aliens brought Elvis Presley back
it looked as if we were under attack
as a mother ship of incredible size
sank down to Earth right in front of our eyes,
and it really gave us an almighty shock
when out of its doors stepped the King of Rock.

There was laughter, tears and celebration,
Elvis is back, he's been on vacation.
There he stood looking leaner and fitter,
Elvis is back, in a suit made of glitter.
It seems the doubters were right all along,
Elvis is back with a dozen new songs.

He's been cutting an album somewhere in space,
now he's bringing it home to the human race.
And the world is listening, holding its breath,
to recordings by Elvis made after his 'death'.

And of course he'd duped us all into thinking
it was pills and burgers and too much drinking
that killed him off, but that wasn't the case,
Elvis escaped to a different place.
He's been touring out there, a star upon stars,
rocking the universe, Venus to Mars.

And as alien ships descend from above
we're sending out our message of love
and hoping they'll show no desire to attack,
but we don't really care because ELVIS IS BACK!

The World's Most Expensive Footballer

The world's most expensive footballer
has credit cards dripping from his fingertips,
his girlfriend tells of his gold-plated lips,
the studs on his boots have diamond tips.

Pound coins fall from his trouser pocket,
under floodlights he glows like a rocket,
he's electrical with no need of a socket,
he's the world's most expensive footballer.

He throws £50 notes to the crowd like confetti,
his finances tangle like a plate of spaghetti,
he's backed an expedition to seek out the Yeti,
he's the world's most expensive footballer.

He dazzles spectators with his fancy passes,
don't stare at him without wearing sunglasses,
all other players his skill surpasses,
he's the world's most expensive footballer.

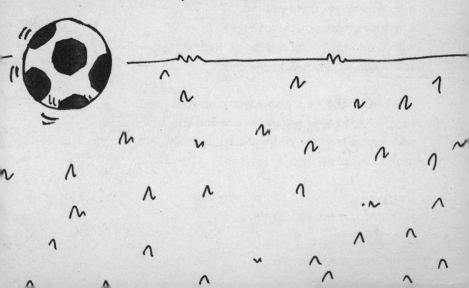

At the Zoo

If you should want to get married at some stage, not right this minute,
but maybe next week . . . you don't have to get married in a church or
at a registry office any more, you can get married on a roller-coaster,
at Wembley Stadium or at London Zoo . . .

If you want to get married at London Zoo
this is what we can offer you . . .

A four metre long reticulated snake
gift-wrapped round your wedding cake.
A choir of hyenas singing loud,
a congregation of apes from rent-a-crowd.
Two charming chimps that will bridesmaid you
and if you need a witness use a kangaroo
at the zoo, at the zoo, at the zoo.

The waiters look great in their penguin suits,
the monkeys will serve you selected fruits.
The alligators are simply delighted,
even ocelots get quite excited.
The Vietnamese pot-bellied pigs
will take to their toes and dance wedding jigs,
at the zoo, at the zoo, at the zoo.

The lions look forward to welcoming you
to your wedding breakfast here at the zoo,
and any leftovers they'd be pleased to chew
at the zoo, at the zoo, at the zoo.

Yes, we look forward to marrying you
at the zoo, at the zoo, at the zoo.

Truants

Mr Flint drove to school each day
with Mrs Brice,
along the way they shared conversation,
shared their troubles, shared petrol money,
and then one day,
one warm bright day at the start of summer,
when the last thing they felt like doing
was teaching troublesome children,
they drove on,
right past the school gates.
Several children saw them,
several children waved
but they took no notice.
They drove on through towns and villages,
past cows and horses at rest on hillsides,
past a windmill, its sails turning lazily
until finally they could travel no more
and ahead of them stretched the sea.
Then they turned and looked at each other
and wondered what they'd done,
but as they'd driven such a long way,
they thought they might as well enjoy themselves.
So they paddled in the sea,
they skipped and chased along the beach,
they flipped stones into the water,
they built a magnificent sandcastle.
For lunch they ate ice cream and candyfloss.
Then they rode a miniature train
to the end of the pier and back,
played a double round of crazy golf,
lost lots of money in amusement arcades

and shared two bags of fish and chips
with a gang of gulls on the prom.

They drove home in silence,
past the horses and cows
and windmill now still
past the school gates
now firmly locked for the night.

And when they sneaked back to school next day
all sheepish and shy,
embarrassed at the fuss they'd caused,
their headteacher
made them go outside at playtime
for a whole week!

THIS IS
THE LIFE

Escape Route

When our teacher came to school today
he looked bright and happy, not old and grey,
not the usual bear whose head was sore,
and we hadn't seen him like this before.
He parked his car in our headteacher's space,
you should have seen the look on her face
as she swept like a hurricane into our room,
and it brightened up our Monday gloom.
But instead of looking a picture of worry
or smiling nervously and saying, sorry
he'd go out and shift it straightaway,
our teacher told her that from today
she could stay and teach his class,
and the look on her face was like frosted glass.

He ripped up test papers in front of her eyes,
then jumped up and down, and to our surprise
planted a slobbery kiss on her cheek,
and just for a moment she couldn't speak,
till he told us how on Saturday night
his lottery numbers had all been right.
Then a noise from outside made us look round
as a helicopter landed in our school grounds,
and our teacher said, 'It's my taxi at last,
this school, all of you, are now in my past.'
Then while we watched, the big blades whirred
and he left for the sky as free as a bird.

And his car is still parked in our headteacher's space.
You should have seen the look on her face!

Licking Toads

'What I want to know is this,'
said Sharon. 'Is kissing Barry Reynolds
worse than licking toads,
or do they rate about the same
on any top ten list of hates?'
So we did a survey, round
all the girls in our year.

'Would you rather the toad or Barry?'
And everyone had to answer
or Sharon threatened to twist
their arms, but Melissa said
it was cruel to go on about Barry,
and we poked fun and said,
'You going to marry him are you?'
And then, when we counted
the votes, it seemed most girls
preferred to chance the toad
than risk kissing Barry.
Sharon said, 'You'd catch less
from the toad.' And then we said,
'Let's try again, would you rather
eat a tarantula egg omelette?'
But no one was quite
so sure about that!

TOAD

What Teachers Wear in Bed!

It's anybody's guess
what teachers wear in bed at night,
so we held a competition
to see if any of us were right.

We did a spot of research,
although some of them wouldn't say,
but it's probably something funny
as they look pretty strange by day.

Our headteacher's quite old fashioned,
he wears a Victorian nightshirt,
our sports teacher wears her tracksuit
and sometimes her netball skirt.

That new teacher in the infants
wears bedsocks with see-through pyjamas,
our deputy head wears a T-shirt
he brought back from the Bahamas.

We asked our secretary what she wore
but she shooed us out of her room,
and our teacher said, her favourite nightie
and a splash of expensive perfume.

And Mademoiselle, who teaches French,
is really very rude,
she whispered, 'Alors! Don't tell a soul,
but I sleep in the . . . back bedroom!

The Lost Angels

In a fish tank in France
we discovered the lost angels,
fallen from heaven and floating now
on imaginary tides.
And all along the sides of the tank,
faces peered, leered at them,
laughing, pouting,
pointing, shouting,
while hung above their heads, a sign,
'Ne pas plonger les mains dans le bassin.'
Don't put your hands in the tank
— the turtles bite seriously.
And who can blame them,
these creatures with angels' wings,
drifting past like alien craft.
Who knows what signals they send
through an imitation ocean,
out of sight of sky,
out of touch with stars?

Dream on, lost angels,
then one day, one glorious day,
you'll flap your wings
and fly again.

The Bonfire at Barton Point

The bonfire at Barton Point
was a wonderful sight, a spectacular blaze,
stuff legends are made of, wicked, ace,
we were talking about it for days.

There were beehives, signboards, slats and tables,
car tyres, a sledge and a wrecked go-cart,
a radiogram with a case of records,
some put-together furniture that must have pulled apart.

And like patients forsaken in mid-operation
there were three-piece suites in states of distress,
gashes in sides, stuffing pulled out,
and a huge Swiss roll of a mattress.

And we knew we'd need some giant of a guy
to lord it over a pile like this,
not a wimp in a baby's pushchair
that the flames would quickly dismiss.

But on the great and glorious night
we found it hard to believe our eyes
as tilted and tumbled onto the fire
came a whole procession of guys.

Then adults took over and just to ensure
the pile of guys would really burn,
they doused the heap with paraffin
so no ghost of a guy could return.

Then matches flared, torches were lit
at several points around the fire
till suddenly everything caught at once
and fingers of flame reached higher.

And beaming guys still peered through smoke
till the fiery serpent wrapped them round
in coils of flame, and they toppled down
to merge with the blazing mound.

With our faces scorched, we turned away,
driven back by waves of heat
till after a time the fire slumped back,
its appetite replete.

Now as long as we live we'll remember
Barton Point with its fiery display
and the charred and blackened treasures
that we pulled from the ashes next day.

HUP

The Whispering Dishes

(At the Science Centre, Herstmonceux Castle)

At the Science Centre
they've positioned
two giant dishes
like satellite receivers,
one hundred metres apart.

Steps lead up to
the centre of each
where a notice reads —

*A whisper at the focus
of one dish
can be heard at the focus
of the other.*

The experiment offers
an immense potential
for acquiring
new scientific knowledge,

a wonderful chance
to develop concepts
of sound transmission.

So what do they do,
what grand words
do children send
to each other
to test out this experiment?

They call out *HELLO*,
then pucker their lips
and blow raspberries!

The Duck Race

There were gales in Humber,
gales in Dogger,
gales in German Bight,

but out on the River Medina,
the water was calm,
the weather was bright

for the Duck Race.
It drove us quackers,
it happened every year.

'Buy a duck,' we were told,
'you may well be in luck.'

And everyone bought,
and everyone hoped
that this year their number
would really come up
on the base of the winning duck.

And Mr Gibbs was
'Master of Ducks',
he took the money
and kept the score.
Then on the day
the race took place
he delivered his ducks
to the river.

He took up position
centre-bridge.
'On your marks, get set,
good luck,' he said,
'and may the best duck win,'
then his parody
of Tennyson was lost
in the noisy din.

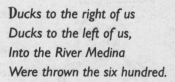

Ducks to the right of us
Ducks to the left of us,
Into the River Medina
Were thrown the six hundred.

And with an almighty splash
of yellow, the ducks hit
the water, then span for a minute
till the current caught them —

some upside down,
some turned round,
some heading back upstream,
some drifting into a whirlpool,
some snagged by
advancing weed.

Some rammed by
a kamikaze duck
and sinking without trace,
some setting the pace
then vanishing,
left to dangle in time and space,
swept from the face of the Earth
by some Bermuda Duck Triangle.

Half the school were panting and yelling,
scrambling down banks and
over bridges, trying to keep
the flotilla in sight
as beak to beak,
tail to tail,
bottom to bottom
and side by side,
the tidal drag of the river
sped ducks to the finishing line.

And it took a photo finish
to decide which duck had won,
but then on its victory paddle
it was blown to smithereens
by a lucky shot from the barrel
of some short-sighted duck hunter's gun!

43

Teachers' Awards

At the end of each summer term
  amid much jollity and back-slapping,
school teachers congratulate each other
  on surviving yet another school year.

So let's hear it for Mrs King,
  the queen of the big production number,
always on a short fuse,
  especially on duty days.

And not forgetting . . . Mr White
  for staying calm when the classroom radiator
leaked rusty water all over
  his recently completed pile of report cards.

Let's hear it for . . . Mrs Salmon,
  who restrained herself quite admirably
when the school gerbil
  ate her winning lottery ticket.

And for Mr Middleton, who has eaten school dinners
  for each day of his twenty-year career,
unable to be with us tonight,
  but we hope he'll be out of hospital soon.

And the romance of the year award
  goes to Miss Buchanan and Mr Duke,
they're dreadfully drippy when they're together,
  it really makes us . . . feel unwell!

And last of all, our dear headmaster,
  who led us all through good times and bad,
till our school inspection came along
  and he suddenly discovered
    a pressing engagement in Barbados.

So let's hear it for those
  fabulous, wonderful creatures,
where would you be without them?
  Let's hear it for THE TEACHERS . . .

Parent-Free Zone

Parents please note that from now on, our room is a 'Parent-Free Zone'.

There will be no spying under the pretence of tidying up.

PARENT FREE ZONE

There will be no banning of television programmes because our room is a tip.

No complaints about noise, or remarks about the ceiling caving in.

No disturbing the dirty clothes that have festered in piles for weeks.

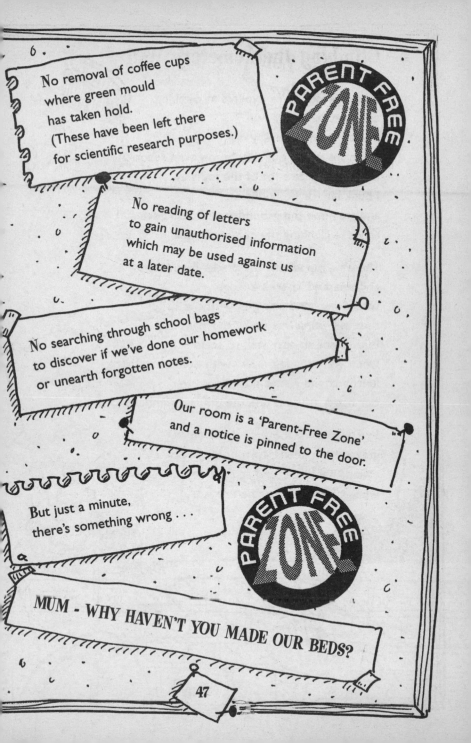

No removal of coffee cups
where green mould
has taken hold.
(These have been left there
for scientific research purposes.)

PARENT FREE ZONE

No reading of letters
to gain unauthorised information
which may be used against us
at a later date.

No searching through school bags
to discover if we've done our homework
or unearth forgotten notes.

Our room is a 'Parent-Free Zone'
and a notice is pinned to the door.

But just a minute,
there's something wrong . . .

PARENT FREE ZONE

MUM - WHY HAVEN'T YOU MADE OUR BEDS?

Climbing the Cemetery Wall

Jake and me, we're experts at climbing
over the cemetery wall.
We do it almost every day
when we steam our way home from school.
It cuts off quite a lot of the journey,
I bunk him or he bunks me,
and we hope the groundsman doesn't see
as we're climbing the cemetery wall.

There's a gap where the bricks have fallen
and smashed, there's a ledge
where we stand and grip with our hands
then pull ourselves up by our nails.
But it's not an easy wall to scale
when we're loaded down with homework books,
lunchbox and games gear slung over
our backs as we tackle the difficult climb.

I've missed my footing lots of times,
grazed both knees, torn holes in clothes,
stained my blazer and scuffed new shoes
while climbing the cemetery wall.

But all in all it's for the best,
it gets us home before anyone else,
though sometimes, if we're late coming out,
there's a lip-curling, fist-whirling
gang of lads whose idea of fun is
fox and hounds, baying like mad
as they hunt us down
while we head for the cemetery wall.

And we haul our bags over the wall
then scramble up as best we can,
but the wall's quite high
and I kneel on my tie, half-strangle
myself till I'm hoisted up
to lie on the top and catch my breath,
or dangle my legs on the other side,
preparing myself for the drop.

I don't suppose the residents mind,
they're pretty quiet much of the time,
though perhaps one or two, when they were alive,
tried climbing the cemetery wall!

Shopping Trolley

Wouldn't it be great to have your own personal shopping trolley that was handed to you the moment you entered a supermarket?

Scoot down the aisles
in my shopping trolley,
I could go for miles
in my shopping trolley.

Never say excuse me,
never say please,
ram it in the back
of someone's knees.

You really won't
believe your eyes,
my shopping trolley's
been customised.

It's got bull bars,
radio controls,
engine in the back
and it purrs like a Rolls.

It's got a Volvo chassis,
a velvet seat,
and around the store
it can't be beat.

It does somersaults
and big backflips,
roly-polys
and wheely dips.

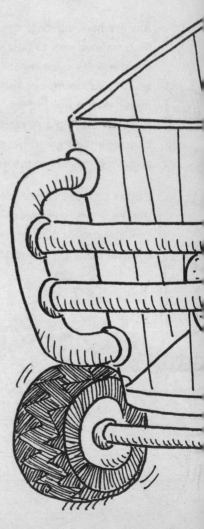

It does over seventy
miles per hour
flashing past
in a burst of power.

*Scoot down the aisles
in my shopping trolley,
I could go for miles
in my shopping trolley.*

Never say excuse me,
never say please,
ram it in the back
of someone's knees.

The World Record Tree Climbing Contest

The world record tree climbing contest
was taking place today,
but Malcolm and me and Ian Gray
we climbed it last night,
though we didn't say,
just left a message pinned to the top:
'Ran out of tree
so we had to stop.'

We couldn't see what the fuss was about,
we'd shinned all sorts of things before,
lamp-posts, cranes, huge whirly slides,
there wasn't much that could stop us.
We'd all climbed out of places too,
when we shouldn't have been inside,
over walls, through windows, down drainpipes,
like regular human flies.

Then later on, with the contest begun,
we sat around to watch the fun, while
fit-looking climbers were kitted up,
padded out at elbows and knees,
tied to each other and strapped to the tree.
But Malcolm and me and Ian Gray
we hadn't bothered with any of that
when we shinned our way to the top.

People cheered and people clapped
while the climbers heaved and grunted and groaned
till they reached their ultimate goal.
Then it must have taken them quite a time
to make some sense out of what we wrote.
Perhaps they couldn't believe what we'd done
but they couldn't deny our note.

Down they came to the ground and then
one of the climbers held up his hand
for silence, and said what he had to say.
The record was off unless anyone knew
the identity of the foolish crew
who climbed the tree late last night,
and to take the record just wouldn't be right.

But Malcolm and me and Ian Gray,
we didn't plan to stake our claim,
we got up whistling and strolled away.
It hadn't been too bad a day
as days go.

Miss Honey

When we first discovered Miss Honey
was to be our new Year Six teacher,
we gaped, mouths open, stopped in our tracks
at the sight of this heaven-sent creature.

She was trim, she was neat, she was lovely
and less than a hundred years old.
She was every fairytale princess
with a smile like liquid gold.

Most of the boys lost their hearts
and would have died for her then and there,
captivated by the pull of her eyes
and the way she flicked back her hair.

They were hooked from the very first moment
she asked them to do her a favour,
they were knights of King Arthur's Round Table
with courage that would never waver.

She wafted between the tables
like a model more used to the catwalk,
while her voice was like honey itself
and we'd much rather listen than talk.

She was wonderful, she was gorgeous,
she was Beauty and we'd been such beasts,
but Miss Honey tamed the wildest class
and all resistance ceased.

Aliens Stole My Underpants

To understand the ways
of alien beings is hard,
and I've never worked it out
why they landed in my backyard.

And I've always wondered why
on their journey from the stars,
these aliens stole my underpants
and took them back to Mars.

They came on a Monday night
when the weekend wash had been done,
pegged out on the line
to be dried by the morning sun.

Mrs Driver from next door
was a witness at the scene
when aliens snatched my underpants –
I'm glad that they were clean!

It seems they were quite choosy
as nothing else was taken.
Do aliens wear underpants
or were they just mistaken?

I think I have a theory
as to what they wanted them for,
they needed to block off a draught
blowing in through the spacecraft door.

COME AND SEE!

Or maybe some Mars museum
wanted items brought back from Space.
Just think, my pair of Y-fronts
displayed in their own glass case.

And on the label beneath
would be written where they got 'em
and how such funny underwear
once covered an Earthling's bottom!

WEIRD!

HA HA
HA

'UNDERPANTS'
FUNCTION:
TO COVER AN
EARTHLING'S 'BOTTOM'

The Wrong Words

We like to sing the wrong words
to Christmas Carols . . .

We three kings of Orient are,
One in a taxi, one in a car . . .

It drives our music teacher barmy,
his face turns red as a holly berry,
his forehead creases, his eyes bulge.
It looks as if the top of his head
is about to lift like a saucepan lid
as he boils over . . .

His anger spills out
in an almighty shout . . .

'NO.' He roars . . .

'If you do that once more
I'll give you the kind of Christmas gift
you won't forget in a hurry . . .'

So we sing . . .

. . . most highly flavoured lady . . .

'IT'S FAVOURED,' he screams
'NOT FLAVOURED . . .

'What do you think she is,
an ice cream cone?'

And then, to cap it all,
and drive him really wild
we sing of the shepherds
washing their socks.

And he slams down the piano lid
and takes off like a rocket
into the stratosphere,
lighting up the sky
like a Christmas star.

Through the Staffroom Door

Ten tired teachers slumped in the staffroom at playtime,
one collapsed when the coffee ran out, then there were nine.

Nine tired teachers making lists of things they hate,
one remembered playground duty, then there were eight.

Eight tired teachers thinking of holidays in Devon,
one slipped off to pack his case, then there were seven.

Seven tired teachers, weary of children's tricks,
one hid in the stock cupboard, then there were six.

Six tired teachers, under the weather, barely alive,
one gave an enormous sneeze, then there were five.

Five tired teachers, gazing at the open door,
one made a quick getaway, then there were four.

Four tired teachers, faces lined with misery,
one locked herself in the ladies', then there were three.

Three tired teachers, wondering what to do,
one started screaming when the bell rang, then there were two.

Two tired teachers, thinking life really ought to be fun,
one was summoned to see the Head, then there was one.

One tired teacher caught napping in the afternoon sun,
fled quickly from the staffroom, then there were none.

- G - O - N - E -

A selected list of poetry books available from Macmillan

The prices shown below are correct at the time of going to press. However, Macmillan Publishers reserve the right to show new retail prices on covers which may differ from those previously advertised.

****

The Secret Lives of Teachers
Poems chosen by Brian Moses   £3.50

More Secret Lives of Teachers
Poems chosen by Brian Moses   £3.50

Aliens Stole My Underpants
Poems chosen by Brian Moses   £2.99

Parent-Free Zone
Poems chosen by Brian Moses   £2.99

Tongue Twisters and Tonsil Twizzlers
Poems chosen by Paul Cookson   £2.99

****

All Macmillan titles can be ordered at your local bookshop or are available by post from:

**Book Service by Post
PO Box 29, Douglas, Isle of Man IM99 1BQ**

Credit cards accepted. For details:
Telephone: 01624 675137
Fax: 01624 670923
E-mail: bookshop@enterprise.net

Free postage and packing in the UK.
Overseas customers: add £1 per book (paperback)
and £3 per book (hardback).